ISBN:978-0-6488890-1-4
Author: Soumaya Arbes Issa
Editor: Umm Marwan Ibrahim
Illustrator: Vector Family
Printed in: China

www.juniorguidance.com

On a Sunday morning, Ali and Asiya woke up early.
"We need to get ready quickly, Asiya. We have lots of things to do today," Ali said excitedly.
Today was the day they would go with their mother to buy decorations for the house.

Ramadan was beginning in a couple of days, and they were all set to welcome it with beautiful ornaments and wall-hangings.

They cleaned their room, finished their breakfast, and got ready in no time to visit the shop in their town.

The store was huge. It was filled with lots of colourful decorations.

There were glow-in-the-dark lanterns, colourful moon lamps, banners and balloons of different sizes, and mini wooden mosques.

Asiya squealed, "Oooh, so many different Ramadan decorations! Where do we begin?!"

Without even realizing it, the kids loaded the whole trolley.

"It's a little much, kids," Mum said, laughing. Even so, she happily paid for it all.

The kids left the store with Mum, talking about where and how they would set the pieces to make the house look spectacular for the month of Ramadan.

On the drive back home, Ali spotted something unusual.

There was a lady sitting on the roadside with a little boy. They were wearing ragged clothes, and their faces looked miserable and sad.

"Mum, what's wrong with them? They look very upset," Ali said with a frown on his face.
"Hmm...Why don't we see what's wrong?"Mum said.

They parked the car close by and Mum stepped out to talk to the lady, while Ali and Asiya watched from the car.

"Are you okay?"Mum asked the lady,"Can we help you in anyway?"

"My son and I haven't eaten since yesterday, sister. We don't have any food at home and we can't afford to buy any," the lady replied in a shaky voice.

Mum excused herself and returned to the car to talk to the kids in private.

"This lady seems to be in real need of food and clothes for herself and her son, kids," she said.

"Now, I don't have any money to give her...unless we return some of the decorations to the store. If we do that, we can then use the money returned to us to buy some food and clothes for them. What do you think?"

Asiya gasped.
"So we won't be decorating the house for Ramadan?! But we were so excited about it...."

"It's okay, Asiya. Some things are more important than decorations," Ali said gently. "I learned at school that when we help someone in need, Allah will reward us in this world and in the hereafter with blessings and gifts beyond our wishes."

"Masha Allah. You're right, Ali." Mum smiled and said to Asiya, "And who said that we won't be decorating the house? We have lots of colourful cardboard at home which we can use to make our own decorations with. And we can have lots of fun while making it."

Asiya's face began to beam again.
"Okay then, let's do it!" she said.

Mum told the lady to wait for them and they left to the store once again.

They returned all of the items except the colourful serial lights.

They visited the grocery, the butchery, and the clothes shop in town and made some quick purchases, before going back to the lady.

"We've got you some food and clothes, aunty. We hope you don't go hungry anymore," Asiya said as they handed her all the stuff they just bought.

With tears in their eyes and smiles on their faces, the lady and her son accepted the bags.
They thanked their friends dearly and made their way home to eat the fresh food and change into the clean clothes they were gifted.

Ali and Asiya were very happy that Allah gave them this opportunity to help someone in need.

When they reached home, the kids gathered all the colourful cardboard pieces they had.
They phoned their friends from the neighbourhood, explained to them what had happened, and sought a hand in creating some homemade decorations.

Many of their neighbourhood friends joined in with pleasure and excitement.
Together, they crafted lanterns, hilals (crescents), mini mosques, and so much more.
They cut letters out of felt to spell "Ramadan Mubarak" and stuck them onto the living room wall.
They also made their very own Ramadan banner.

After a couple of hours and lots of chatter and fun, the decorations were finally completed.
The house looked bright and colourful.
And there were still some excess decorations, which Ali and Asiya decided to share with their friends.

Mubarak

"Hey, there's still a few blank cardboard pieces we haven't used," Asiya remarked, "Let's make something extra special with them."
"Hmm...I have an idea! Let's make banners where we write 'Ramadan Mubarak' in our different languages."

"That's awesome!" their friends cheered.
Kids of different native countries, each drew a little flag of their homeland on a banner and wrote "Ramadan Mubarak" on it in their language. Arabic, Azerbaijani, Russian, Hindi, and Turkish were among them.

रमजान मुबारक

Ramazan ay mubarek olsun

Рамадан Му

By the time the banners were done, it was 3 o'clock.
Everybody helped Ali and Asiya clean up the mess they had made and left
feeling eager to decorate their own houses for Ramadan.

Ramazan Mübarak

رمضان مبارك

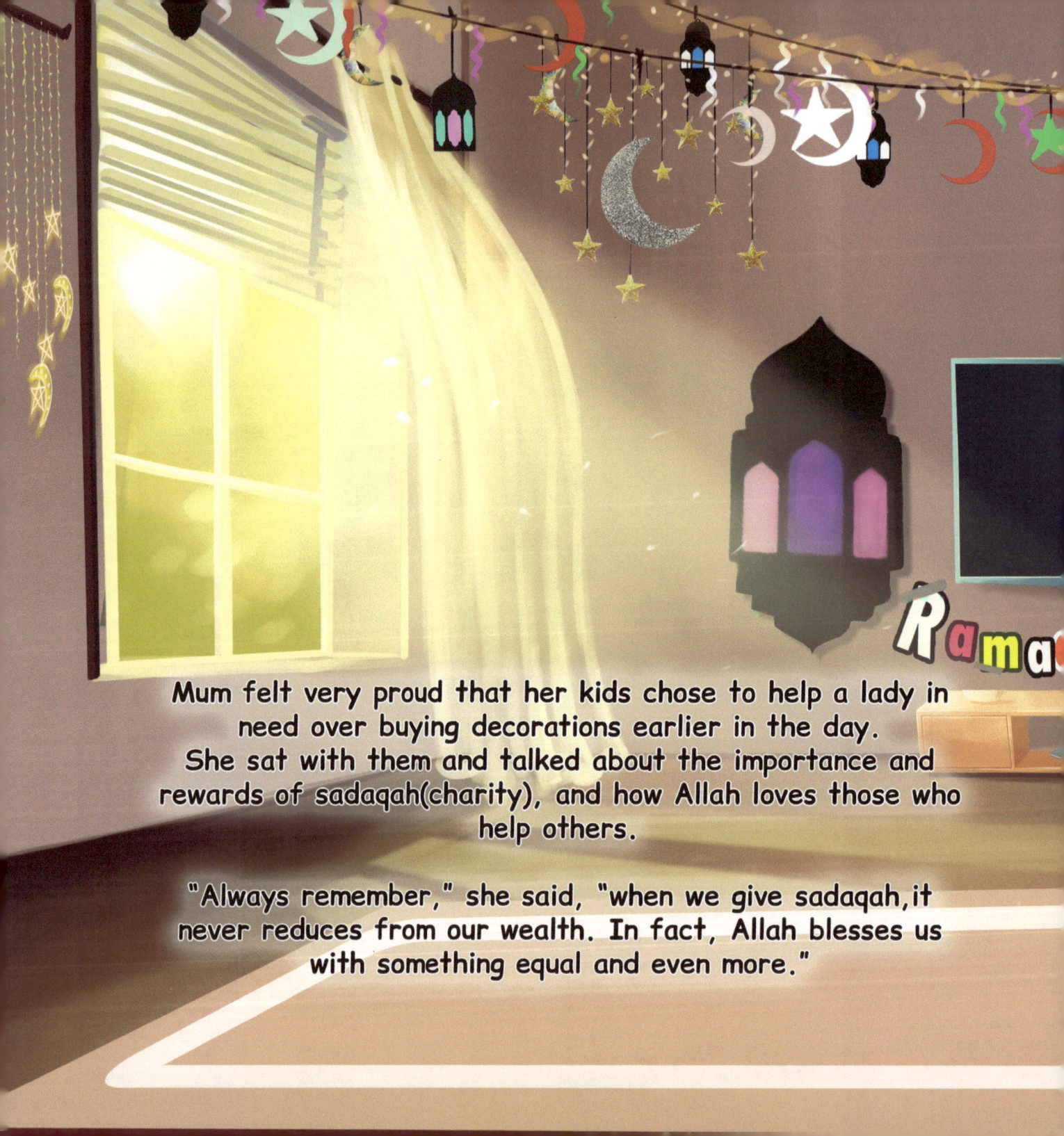

Mum felt very proud that her kids chose to help a lady in
need over buying decorations earlier in the day.
She sat with them and talked about the importance and
rewards of sadaqah(charity), and how Allah loves those who
help others.

"Always remember," she said, "when we give sadaqah, it
never reduces from our wealth. In fact, Allah blesses us
with something equal and even more."

"Tell me, kids. Did you enjoy today?" she asked.
They nodded cheerfully.

"We had so much fun with everyone, Mum!" Asiya said.
"Yeah, it was so good to have all our friends come over and help us make cool decorations from scratch," Ali pitched in.

"Alhamdulillah. This is how Allah has rewarded you for your sacrifice, my lovelies. Not only did you get to enjoy the company of your friends, but you also got your Ramadan decorations handmade with extra love and care. And you got this blessing from Allah only by making someone else in need happy."

Ali and Asiya smiled, thrilled to know that Allah would be pleased with them.

Meanwhile, on the other side of town, the poor lady and her son were content.
They had a meal that filled their tummies and clean new clothes to wear.

They thanked Allah for sending them someone to help, and made lots of dua to Allah to protect and always keep their helpers safe and at peace.

The end

# DID YOU KNOW?

• Ramadan is the 9th month in the Islamic calendar, when Muslims fast (keep away from eatingand drinking) from dawn until sunset.

• The Quran was revealed in Ramadan on the Night of Decree (known as 'LaylatulQadr')

• LaylatulQadr is the night when the Quran was first sent down from the heavens to the earth.It is also the night when the first verses of the Quran were revealed to our beloved Prophet Muhammed (peace be upon him).

• In the month of Ramadan, rewardsaregreatly multiplied. That is why Muslims strive to do lots of good deeds in that month, such as praying taraweeh (special voluntary prayer of Ramadan) at night, giving charity, and inviting family and friends over for feasts.

• Allah says in the Quran: "Those who spend in charity will be richly rewarded." (57:10)

• He also says:"Truly, Allah does reward the charitable." (12:88)

• Prophet Muhammed (peace be upon him) said: "Protect yourself from hellfire even by giving a piece of date as charity." (Narrated byal-Bukhari and Muslim )

• He (peace be upon him) also said: "Charity extinguishes sin, just as water extinguishes fire." (Narrated by Tirmidhi)

www.ingramcontent.com/pod-product-compliance
Lightning Source LLC
Chambersburg PA
CBHW041432090426
42741CB00028B/81